Read All About
Horses

QUARTER HORSES

LYNN M. STONE

The Rourke Corporation, Inc.
Vero Beach, Florida 32964

PHOTO CREDITS:
© Lynn M. Stone: cover, pages 4, 6, 7, 10, 19, 21, 22; courtesy of American Quarter Horse Association: pages 9, 12, 13, 15, 16; © William Munoz: page 18

EDITORIAL SERVICES:
Penworthy Learning Systems

Library of Congress Cataloging-in-Publication Data

Stone, Lynn M.
    Quarter horses / Lynn M. Stone.
        p. cm. — (Horses)
    Includes index.
    Summary: Describes the history and physical characteristics of the oldest all-American horse breed, the quarter horse.
    ISBN 0-86593-514-9
    1. Quarter horse—Juvenile literature. [1. Quarter horse. 2. Horses.]
I. Title II. Series: Stone, Lynn M. Horses.
SF293.Q3S73 1998
636.1'33—dc21   98–25097
                                                                        CIP
                                                                        AC

Printed in the USA

TABLE OF CONTENTS

THE QUARTER HORSE

The quarter horse is the oldest all-American **breed** (BREED). Early quarter horses date back to the 1600s.

The quarter horse earned its name by running extremely fast over one-quarter-mile (about half a kilometer) race courses.

The quarter horse has become one of the world's most popular breeds, or types, of horse. It is quick, but it is also **versatile** (VER suh til). It can be used for many purposes. Among other uses, the quarter horse is a fine, good-natured trail horse.

The popular quarter horse earned its reputation—and name—as a quick quarter-miler.

THE FIRST QUARTER HORSES

In early America, horses were largely Spanish types. They had been brought to the New World by Spanish explorers.

During the 1600s, English settlers brought English horse breeds to America. They often raced their horses over short distances.

The quarter horse has many skills, but talking isn't one of them.

The quarter horse has become a breed for all seasons.

The settlers soon decided to cross their English horses with the smaller, quicker Spanish horses. The result was a better horse and the beginning of the quarter horse.

HISTORY OF THE QUARTER HORSE

In the early 1800s, the English thoroughbred was imported by Americans. The thoroughbred was a great distance racer. Racing interest in America quickly switched from the short courses to longer courses. The quarter horse was no match for a thoroughbred on a long course.

The interest in quarter horses faded in the East. But quarter horses increased in number in the West. Owners found that the quarter horse could pull buggies, wagons, and plows. It could also stop and start quickly. That's exactly the kind of horse the cowboys needed to chase cattle.

A quarter horse is often the horse of choice for riding on western trails.

THE QUARTER HORSE BODY

The handsome quarter horse's coat may be a shade of brown, black, gray, or even the creamy color known as **palomino** (pal uh MEE no). Quarter horses often have white trim on the face and legs.

The bridge of the quarter horse's nose is usually straight. It has a slightly arched neck. A quarter horse has small ears and lively eyes.

Quarter horses weigh up to about 1,200 pounds (545 kilograms). They stand from 14 to 16 **hands** (HANDZ) high (about five feet, or one to two meters).

A palomino quarter horse waits patiently for its rider at a hitching rail in Colorado.

QUARTER HORSES IN AMERICA

With the end of quarter-mile racing in the East, the quarter horse became more of a western horse. There the quarter horse became the favorite trail horse and cow pony.

The quarter horse can start and stop, its owners say, "on a dime."

Quarter horse owners have a chance to compete in many events, like barrel racing, at AQHA shows.

Today the American Quarter Horse Association is the largest horse breed organization ever. It lists nearly 3,000,000 **registered** (REJ iss terd) quarter horses. Each year the AQHA approves more than 2,400 quarter horse shows for its members worldwide.

GROWING UP A QUARTER HORSE

Quarter horse babies are known as **foals** (FOLZ). Their mothers are mares.

The mare raises her foal on mother's milk for about five months. Meanwhile, the foal has also begun to nibble grass and hay.

The foal's father, called a **stallion** (STAL yun), has no part in raising his offspring.

By the age of two or three years, the young quarter horse is ready for a saddle and rider.

A quarter horse mare (left) raises her foal on mother's milk.

QUARTER HORSES AT WORK

The quarter horse was developed by horse **breeders** (BREE derz) to race. Many quarter horses are still used in one-quarter mile (about a half kilometer) races. Such races have become, once again, quite popular.

Quarter horses are outstanding trail and rodeo horses, too. Quarter horses compete in several rodeo events, including calf roping and barrel racing.

Quarter horses are also used for jumping and even the demanding riding events of **dressage** (dreh SAHJH).

Quarter horses are the most popular riding horses in America.

QUARTER HORSES ON THE RANGE

Beef cattle are raised in the rangelands of the West. This rugged, open land is quarter horse country.

The quarter horse has speed, balance, and sure movements. These abilities make this breed a natural cow pony.

A quarter horse and rider hold a tight rope during calf branding in Montana.

Florida ranchers use quarter horses for much of their cattle roundup work.

The quarter horse, cowboys like to say, "just seems to know what to do" when it's working with cattle.

QUARTER HORSE COUSINS

All horses are cousins of each other. Some, however, are more closely linked than others.

Thoroughbreds, for example, are similar to quarter horses in size and build. And the breeds share a love for running, too.

Thoroughbreds are often crossed with quarter horses. Their offspring are mixed breeds—a mix of quarter horse and thoroughbred.

A quarter horse-thoroughbred mix usually has more speed over distance than a **purebred** (PEUR bred) quarter horse.

Thoroughbreds are the world's finest and fastest racing horses over mid-length and long-distance tracks.

GLOSSARY

breed (BREED) — a particular group of domestic animals having the same characteristics, such as shape or color

breeder (BREE der) — one who raises animals, such as horses, and lets them reproduce

dressage (dreh SAHJH) — complex moves by a horse in response to a rider's shifting weight

foal (FOL) — a horse before the age of one year

hand (HAND) — a four-inch (ten-centimeter) measure of horses' shoulder height

palomino (pal uh MEE no) — any breed of horse with a cream-colored coat and light tail and mane

purebred (PEUR bred) — a domestic, or tame, animal made up entirely of a single (pure) breed

registered (REJ iss terd) — listed officially in a book (register) as part of a specific breed

stallion (STAL yun) — an adult male horse that can father foals

versatile (VER suh til) — able to do many things well

Gentle and good natured, quarter horses have a variety of talents.

23

INDEX

FURTHER READING

Find out more about horses with this helpful organization:

American Quarter Horse Association, P.O. Box 200, Amarillo, TX 79168,
   telephone: 1-800-414-RIDE or online at—http://www.aqha.com